MW01710504

Steps to Heaven

Joe Crews

ONE
THE DIAGNOSIS

If there could be a highway to the moon, it would take 20 months of constant driving at the rate of 400 miles per day to reach the land of the moon. If there could be a railroad stretching up to the sun, a streamlined train traveling 90 mph nonstop, day after day and year after year, would require 116 years to reach sunny land. An airplane flying at 500 mph would have to travel nonstop for 500 years to reach the nearest fixed star.

Yet far beyond the starry sky lie the pearly gates of God's great heavenly sky city. No one knows how far it is in miles, and no one will ever develop a space vehicle for going there, but every one of us can get to that beautiful place by taking three simple steps that we're going to talk about in this little book.

In the book of Revelation, John declared that "nothing which defileth" would go through the gates into that dwelling place of God. The only thing that defiles in God's sight is sin. Isaiah wrote, "your iniquities have separated between you and your God" (Isaiah 59:2). In order to live again in the presence of God, each individual must be free from the condemnation brought on by sin. The apostle John confirmed this fact by his description of that great multitude that he saw in vision standing before the throne of God. They had palms in their hands and were dressed in white robes, representing freedom from sin (Revelation 7:9).

So mark it down as the first giant step on the way from earth to heaven: we must have our *sins forgiven.* This is probably the best-known fact about the entire salvation process. Yet the most perplexing questions are raised about the way to take this step. The truth is that millions have only the vaguest idea about how to obtain relief from the guilt of their wrongdoing. How can a person obtain pardon and be restored to a saving union with God?

It is my belief that countless numbers of people really want to be Christians, but no one has made it clear enough or appealing enough to win their decision. In the next few pages you will read the most simple, bottom-line explanation of the plan of salvation. Even the children should be able to understand what it means to be saved. I do not believe that it is enough to just tell people they are lost and need to be found. We must show them step by step how to pass from death to life. The doctor doesn't tell his patients that they are sick and need to be well without giving a prescription for their healing. In the same way, we must be prepared to offer a specific cure for those who have been diagnosed with the disease of sin.

TWO
CONDITIONS OF FORGIVENESS

Now let's take a closer look at this first step marked *Sins Forgiven.* How does one obtain the requisite pardon for those sins that have become such a common lot for every human being? We need to understand from the very beginning that there are three conditions to having our sins forgiven—repentance, confession, and restitution. Please do not let those long theological terms confuse you. We shall break them into such simple language that all will know what they mean and how to fulfill their requirements.

What about the first condition? What is repentance, and what are we to repent of? The Bible says, "All have sinned and come short of the glory of God" (Romans 3:23). The meaning of these inspired words is very clear. Regardless of our wealth, sex, or station in life we have all made personal choices to break God's law. The Bible calls it sin. No resolute human effort has been sufficient to overcome the inherited tendencies to have our own way. The results of that original sin by Adam and Eve have been passed along to every succeeding generation, ours included. The inability to meet God's standard is a part of the carnal nature that has marked every member of the human family since the fall of our first parents.

We can better understand how "all have sinned" when we look at the beautiful, innocent little baby throwing a tantrum when its will is crossed. There is no age when the fallen nature has power of itself to control the life and modify the behavior. The Bible declares, "The carnal mind … is not subject to the law of God, neither indeed can be" (Romans 8:7). Jeremiah made the interesting observation: "Can the Ethiopian change his skin, or the leopard his spots? then may ye also do good, that are accustomed to do evil" (Jeremiah 13:23).

In other words, not one of us has the ability to change this lost and dying condition into which we have been thrust. We cannot lift ourselves by our own bootstraps. Not even education, culture, or any of the other amenities of society are able to reverse the consequences of our sinful heritage.

After recognizing the fact that our yielding to the propensities of our genetic natures has condemned us all, we are next confronted with the result of our transgressions. Paul describes it very succinctly in these words: "The wages of sin is death" (Romans 6:23). With this shocking line, the full horror of our situation appears before us. Not only are we all guilty, but we also have been sentenced to die for our sins. Every member of the human family is consigned to a death-row status as a consequence of our willful disobedience.

Is it not more than alarming to be confronted with our own death sentence, realizing that there is not a court or judge in the universe that will declare us "not guilty"? The fact is, of course, that we are just as guilty as sin. Furthermore, the penalty is absolutely irreversible, and God Himself could not cancel it without contradicting His own character and law.

Is there a solution to our dilemma? Someone may suggest that our only recourse is to go ahead and pay the penalty for what we have done wrong. By dying for our sins, we can uphold the justice of God and satisfy the demands of a broken law at the same time. We could do that all right, but where would it leave us? Since we have no power to raise ourselves from the dead, we would be eternally cut off from life, with no hope of a resurrection. Certainly that course does not seem to be a very satisfactory answer to our problem.

Finally, we have to face the truly disturbing fact that we owe something we cannot pay. We owe our very lives for our sin-debt and have no way to pay without forfeiting all future existence. It is as though a man bought all of his month's groceries on credit and then had no way to settle the $200.00 account at the end of the month. Out of embarrassment and shame, the man avoided the store with his delinquent account. But then his best friend heard about the poor man's financial problem. Immediately the friend went to the store and counted out the full $200.00 to settle the account. Wasn't that a wonderful act of friendship and love? Now the man has no reason for feeling shame or guilt. The debt has been paid. His record is clear. What would you think of that reprieved man if he had refused the kindly act of his friend? Would it not be a gross insult to the one who made such a magnanimous gesture?

Now let's apply that little story to our own case. We also owe something we can't pay—our very lives. But a friend, in the person of Jesus, says: "I will assume your debt, suffer death in your place, and put it all to the credit of your personal account."

That offer stands behind all three of the steps we are considering in the salvation experience. It constitutes the basis of our receiving forgiveness for our sins. How is the guilt, condemnation, and death sentence transferred from you and me and placed upon Jesus, our divine Substitute? The answer to that question brings us back to the three conditions for taking the big step of obtaining forgiveness. The first condition is *Repentance.*

THREE
WHAT IS REPENTANCE?

I promised to simplify that long theological word. It literally means to feel a godly sorrow for the wrongs we have committed. Such genuine sorrow is only possible when we fully recognize that our only hope rests in the death of Jesus on the cross in our place. Helplessly we must turn away from self and "behold the Lamb of God," who takes away the sin of the world. What happens as we watch Him bleeding, suffering, and dying on the cross? We realize that He was holy and innocent. We were the guilty ones. We should be hanging there instead of Him. We are overwhelmed to realize that He would have submitted to the torture and death for only one soul, even for you or me. Suddenly our eyes fill with tears as we realize that our sins caused His death on the cross. His heart was broken by the crushing weight of sins that had been taken from us. He was voluntarily suffering the punishment we deserved. We are filled with *sorrow* that we ever committed those very sins that now are taking the life of the Son of God. *That sorrow is repentance.*

We must clearly distinguish between a worldly sorrow and a genuine godly sorrow. Sometimes children say, "I'm sorry" when facing punishment for misbehavior, but often they are merely regretful that they got caught. This is not true repentance. When I was in high school one of my teachers was the sports coach. He was a nice enough fellow, but not a very effective communicator. Therefore, it was a treat when a young lady teacher took his place in the middle of the school year. All of us boys were especially delighted because this new teacher was very pretty and not much older than some of us.

In the beginning, we were vying for her attention in ways that were probably very distracting to everyone. One day I stayed after school with two friends to play some basketball. Later, after all the other students had left, we went by our room to pick up our books. Just before opening the door, we glanced through the one clear pane of glass in the door and there we saw our beautiful girl-teacher weeping at her desk. No one needed to tell us why she was crying, because we instantly remembered some of the things we had done during classes. None of us had any desire to hurt that teacher. We liked her very much and had no idea that we were causing her so much grief. We were sick and ashamed of ourselves that day, and it was three very sorry boys who crept down the hall without opening that door. All three of us made a covenant that day that we would never do anything again that would hurt our pretty young teacher. We were truly repentant.

This same principle applies to those who feel sorrow for the pain their sins caused Jesus to suffer, and by God's grace they determine to turn away from everything displeasing to Him.

FOUR
Why Should We Confess?

The second condition of forgiveness is called *Confession.* John wrote, "If we confess our sins, he is faithful and just to forgive us our sins, and to cleanse us from all unrighteousness" (1 John 1:9). That certainly sounds simple enough. Yet it is on this point that most people stumble and lose their way. The question most commonly asked is this: How do I know I have been forgiven? There is only one correct answer to that question. We know we are forgiven because God said we would be. Here is where the beautiful element of faith comes into the picture. We have every reason to know that God's Word cannot ever fail. Whatever it says will take place.

There is built-in, self-fulfilling power in every promise of the Bible.

Could the man lame from birth stand upon his feet? No, it was impossible. He was carried every day to beg outside the temple in Jerusalem. Yet Peter commanded, "In the name of Jesus Christ of Nazareth, rise up and walk" (Acts 3:6). Suppose the man had remained on his pallet and said to Peter, "I can't even stand on my feet, much less walk or run. I've been crippled all my life, and have no strength in my feet to move off this bed." Do you think he would have been healed? No, he had to accept as a fact that Jesus of Nazareth had strengthened those anklebones so that he could get up and walk. When he made the effort as though his feet were normal, they were restored to normal. "According to your faith so be it unto you."

You may not *feel* forgiven when you ask for it, but the promise is that you *are* forgiven. So forget about feeling. Believe that it's done because God said it would be. Thank Him for it and then act like it's done, because it is. Your faith makes it a fact.

Someone might say, "Well, I thought Christians got happy feelings as a result of accepting Jesus." Let me assure you, that feeling will follow as a *result* of your faith and forgiveness, but always remember that faith must come before feeling. Paul had it right when he wrote, "Therefore being justified by faith, we have peace with God through our Lord Jesus Christ" (Romans 5:1). Just imagine for a moment that feeling came before faith in forgiveness. In that case you would be a peaceful, joyful unbeliever, and there is no such creature as that.

By the way, what is the real secret behind the confession process? Why do we need to tell God about our mistakes and sins? Doesn't He already know without my recounting them to Him? Of course, it is true that we do not inform God about anything He doesn't know already. Our confession does not change Him either; it changes us. Ask anyone who has been courageous enough to ask forgiveness. You can probably remember having to make something right with an individual in the past. Perhaps you had repeated some exaggerated rumor about the person and he found out that you were responsible. Even though it was hard, you gathered up your courage and stammered out your apology. What happened immediately? You felt as though a great weight had rolled off your shoulders. Tremendous relief flooded your soul. Yet, you told that person nothing that he didn't know before. He was already fully aware of your words that brought him so much pain. You needed that confession more than he did.

FIVE
RESTITUTION

The third condition to having our sins forgiven is *Restitution*. This long word simply means that we make every effort to correct the things we have done wrong. Of course, we recognize that it is never possible to reach into the past and rectify every wrong, every lie, and every dishonest act. In the first place, we can't even remember all the times we were guilty of those things. It would probably drive a person insane to feel the responsibility for such an impossible demand. Nevertheless, the Spirit probes our consciences and reminds us of the matters that can be made right.

If something has been stolen, it certainly should be restored. If lies have been told which damaged someone's reputation, we can apologize and tell the truth in order to remove any stigma on that person's character. Sometimes prison might be a possible consequence if crimes of theft or robbery have been committed, but it is very important to arrange repayment whenever the possibility exists. In cases where restitution is not possible, the repentant one can safely trust the cleansing merits of Christ's blood to provide pardon and restoration.

Is it difficult to confront and correct our past sins? Indeed, it is probably the most excruciating part of the redemptive process. This may explain why so many have convinced themselves that it is not a biblical requirement. But might it not also provide a partial explanation as to why spiritual renewal has been so elusive in the modern church? Many believe that a tremendous revival would sweep the Christian churches if every member made genuine restitution to those they have wronged.

Meeting the three conditions of repentance, confession, and restitution brings assurance that the longest step has been taken in becoming a true Christian. The sins are now forgiven and can no longer crush the conscience with guilt. Here is where we encounter the real answer to the question about the transfer of sin onto the divine Substitute. When we reach out in faith, believing that He truly has taken our place on the cross, a very marvelous transaction is consummated. The death penalty that rested upon us is instantly removed from us and placed on Jesus. It is exactly as though we were with Him on the cross suffering the required sentence, and yet, we were only there by faith. He experienced the pain and punishment for us, but because we confess Him as our Saviour, He actually treats us as though we ourselves had died and paid the penalty for our own guilty acts.

But not only does God accept the atoning sacrifice of His Son as a total satisfaction of the universal death sentence against every member of the fallen race, He imputes to each one who chooses to accept it the credit for living a life just as holy as Jesus lived. In other words, they are not only declared "not guilty"; they are declared to be just as righteous as the sinless Saviour who lived here in the flesh for 33 years without committing a single sin. It is in this amazing manner that all degrees of transgression are canceled, and "whosoever will" may stand without condemnation before God. His faith alone has opened a door to a new "standing" in relation to God. It is called justification, and it provides forgiveness for every wrongdoing of the past that has been repented of, confessed, and forsaken. And even though it can be said that the death of Jesus, in one sense, made a corporate reconciliation of all men to God, it is only through personal acceptance of the sacrifice that anyone can experience "justification by faith."

Does the totality of salvation, then, consist of a mere "accounting" on the part of God? Is our part only to *believe* that God does everything for us, and then wait for Him to waft us on rose-tinted clouds into the kingdom of heaven? Indeed not. So far, we have described that part of righteousness by faith that flows from outside ourselves. It is called justification and is based wholly upon the objective acts of God in our behalf. It is true that we cannot work for this imputed credit for being righteous. We can only accept the atoning merits of the blood of Jesus, which bears witness that somebody else paid the penalty for our sins. By exercising faith in this divine Substitute, who took our place in death, we acquire a certain "standing" of righteousness before God.

But it is most necessary that we understand that God does not ascribe some legal fiction to us by calling us righteous when we really are not. Righteousness by faith includes more than just a "standing" or "accounting." God not only imputes righteousness to us through justification to take care of our past sins, but He imparts righteousness to us through sanctification to keep us from future sins. In other words, there is a "state" of righteousness before God as well as a "standing" of being righteous. We'll have more to say about these two aspects of righteousness by faith as we move into the next chapter. Keep in mind, though, that whether imputed or imparted, all true righteousness originates with God and resides in us only as long as Christ abides in us through faith.

SIX
THE NECESSITY OF THE NEW BIRTH

Now we are prepared to consider the second large step in this exciting, journey from earth to heaven, and it is very closely tied to the faith transaction we have considered. That moment of acceptance not only brings an objective change of standing before God, but it also produces a fantastic subjective transformation in the heart and mind of the believer. Jesus referred to this dramatic experience as being "born of the Spirit." The necessity of it was revealed in the urgent words of the Master to Nicodemus, "Except a man be born again, he cannot see the kingdom of God" (John 3:3).

There is no possible way to analyze or diagnose the miraculous, and often instantaneous, change that accompanies this act of faith. The apostle John seems to express it as simply as it can be communicated: "But as many as received him, to them gave he power to become the sons of God, even to them that believe on his name" (John 1:12). But even though we can't understand the mystery, we can observe the results of it very clearly. Paul described it in these words. "Therefore if any man be in Christ, he is a new creature: old things are passed away; behold, all things are become new" (2 Corinthians 5:17).

Like a gentle brush of the invisible wind, God's Holy Spirit enters the life to replace the surrendered fleshly things with the exact opposite. Although the inherent fallen nature is not removed by the new birth, the carnal mind is replaced with a spiritual mind that has the power to subdue all the desires and passions that might arise from that fallen nature. It is this progressive work of conquering self and constantly submitting the will to Christ which leads us to the third giant step on our heavenly pilgrimage. We call it *sanctification.*

Again when we reduce this long theological word to its elementary meaning, all confusion evaporates. It simply means loving obedience to all of God's revealed will. The word "loving" distinguishes those acts of obedience from the legalistic forced conformity of those who might be trying to earn salvation by mere law keeping. Some liberal-minded religionists equate obedience and legalism. They ignore the difference between heart service and head service. One is the very finest demonstration of true religion and the other shows forth the most dangerous counterfeit. Someone has suggested that millions will miss heaven by just eighteen inches-the distance from the head to the heart. Complying with God's law in order to fulfill a legal requirement for salvation is the head approach, but true heart obedience is the spontaneous outflow of a personal love relationship with Christ.

When we talk about sanctification here, we are referring solely to the heart approach.

There has been much debate over the way justification and sanctification relate to each other, so let's clarify it with a few simple observations. We need both of these experiences in order to be ready for heaven. Justification imputes the perfect victory of Jesus to cover our past sins, but sanctification imparts the victorious power of Jesus to preserve us from committing further sin. We can't have one without the other. Anyone who exercises true faith is justified. All who are truly justified are converted, or turned into a new creation; and all who have experienced the new birth will walk in obedience out of love. The cause-effect is instantaneous and inseparable. There is no justification without sanctification and no sanctification without justification. Nevertheless, it is very important to keep in mind that justification, as the very first approach to God, is freely bestowed and is not granted in reference to our good works. This biblical principle requires that the believer receive the gift of justification *before* sanctified obedience is possible. Then the conformity to the law is recognized as the result of the born-again connection with the Saviour.

As you have probably realized by now, there are many professed Christians who consider step number three to be optional in the salvation experience. But unless we ignore many plain statements of scripture, it is impossible for us to come to such a conclusion. The Bible says, "And being made perfect, he became the author of eternal salvation unto all them that obey him" (Hebrews 5:9). Obedience is truly one of the spiritual requirements for entrance into the kingdom. John declared that "there shall in no wise enter into it anything that defileth" (Revelation 21:27).

Sin, of course, is the only thing that defiles in God's sight, and it is specifically excluded from entering the gates of Paradise. Sin is defined in the Bible as transgression of the law. This means there will be no thieves, murderers, adulterers, etc., in heaven. Should it frighten us to learn that willful sin must be put away in order to be saved? Incidentally, we are not saying here that the good works of obedience are the grounds for our acceptance by Jesus, but they are the necessary accompaniment of a freely bestowed gift to all who believe.

None who have accepted that gift will be discouraged by the requirement to stop deliberately transgressing the revealed will of God. Converted hearts are eager to please the One they love supremely. They delight to walk in obedience because God's law has been written into their hearts and minds.

Why is it easier for most Christians to take the first two steps of the three we have dealt with so far? Is it because forgiveness and conversion are largely accomplished for us and in us by the power of God in response to our faith alone, while sanctification demands strong effort in addition to our faith? It is entirely possible. For that reason, I want to share, in the next few paragraphs, the greatest secret I ever learned about living the Christian life. How does one turn away from sins that are rooted in strong physical or psychological addiction? What about smoking, alcoholism, and drugs?

SEVEN
CLAIMING THE VICTORY—SANCTIFICATION

Total victory over all sin has been promised through scores of Bible texts, but four of them will suffice to bring deliverance to every one who will claim them in faith. May I address you personally about your besetting weakness, problem, or addiction? The simple, practical steps you are about to learn could make the difference between life and death in your future. Let nothing divert you from this biblical formula that is guaranteed to break any chain or habit in your life that you are willing to relinquish.

The first text contains a most important principle about victory over sin. "But thanks be to God, which giveth us the victory through our Lord Jesus Christ" (1 Corinthians 15:57). May this glorious truth grip your mind. Victory is a *gift!* It is not something you can earn or deserve. Neither is it bestowed as a reward for hard effort and struggle. It is freely granted to those who ask for it in the right way. But, you may inquire, what is the right way to ask God for this gift? The answer is contained in just one *word—faith.* Jesus said, "According to your faith so be it unto you." Everything promised in the Bible is yours for the asking, but you must believe it in order to receive it.

Now let's illustrate that principle by moving to the second text. "If ye then, being evil, know how to give good *gifts* unto your children, how much more shall your Father which is in heaven give good things to them that *ask* him" (Matthew 7:11, emphasis added)? Notice that this verse is also talking about asking for gifts, and the previous text told us that the gift is "victory" over sin. From these words of Jesus, we learn that His Father is more willing and eager to give us the "good things" we ask for than we are to feed our children when they are hungry!

Next question: "Is victory a good thing to ask for?" Of course, and victory is also a "gift," as we were told in 1 Corinthians 15:57. And on the authority of Jesus' own words, if we ask for this good gift, God will give it more freely than loving parents would feed their children.

By the way, we don't even have to incorporate the phrase "If it be Thy will" into this prayer request, because the Bible already assures us that it is His will to free us from all sin. If we were asking for some physical gift, such as healing or a better job, we would certainly have to include that phrase in our prayer.

We are now prepared to make an observation. Whatever gift of victory over sin you ask for, it will be immediately bestowed. *If you do not believe that with your whole heart, then do not pursue this plan any further.* If you do believe victory will be yours the moment you ask, then drop on your knees and ask Him now, calling the sin by name. As you rise from your knees you will not feel that anything has changed, but your feelings have nothing to do with it. A wonderful thing has happened. The instant you prayed, God placed a mighty reservoir of power into your life. That power is the victory over your sin! You have it now!

Some might ask, "How can I know the victory has been given?" Simply because God promised to give it when you asked

Him. In some cases God actually removes the taste or desire for the activity, but that is not the usual way He does it. The appetite may remain strong in the majority of those who seek deliverance, but they still have the power from God never to yield to that craving again. The secret is to accept without question that what God promised has indeed taken place.

Do you remember how Peter walked on the water? Jesus assured him that he could do it, and the big fisherman stepped out of the boat and began to do the impossible. Nobody can walk on water, but Peter did it—for a while. How long did he do it? The Bible says the wind and the waves were boisterous, and he became afraid. What was he afraid of? Obviously, of sinking and drowning. But didn't that doubt the word of Jesus? The Master had told Peter that he could come to Him.

In the same way, He has promised to give us the victory as a gift. He invites us to come to Him. What should our response be? Whatever our spiritual infirmity, we should "step out of the boat" and affirm that we have power from God never to yield to that sin again. We can tell anybody or everybody that God has set us free, and we no longer are bound by that habit. Our faith will grow as we bear witness to what God has done, and also as we constantly thank and praise Him for the gift of victory.

Paul wrote: "Likewise reckon ye also yourselves to be dead indeed unto sin" (Romans 6:11). These are the most important words for those following the faith plan of overcoming. The word "reckon" means to count it as done. There must be no reservation in considering the sin as "dead" on the basis of God's promise. Our greatest temptation, at this point, is to think about the many times we have tried and failed to put this sin out of our lives. Satan will attack our faith by suggesting that we cannot possibly survive without indulging this particular sin, and that we are much too weak to give it up. Our greatest test will be to overwhelm and drown that "trying" argument of the self-nature and focus by faith on God's gift-plan of total victory.

EIGHT
FAITH MAKES NO PROVISION TO FAIL

The final text in claiming deliverance is found in Romans 13:14: "But put ye on the Lord Jesus Christ, and make not provision for the flesh to fulfil the lusts thereof." This lays the final timber in God's foolproof, perfect plan of giving the victory. How can a dead person lay plans to keep sinning? If you knew you would be dead tomorrow morning, would you make any provisions for tomorrow afternoon? If you "reckon yourself dead" to any sin through the power of the Word, it would be a contradiction of nature to act as though the sin was still in control. It would also be a denial of the promise of God. If He says you have the victory, believe it!

Now we have clearly before us the uncomplicated scheme of salvation as it has been described in the Bible. The three big steps are *Sins Forgiven*, *New Birth*, and *Obedience*. Every child, youth, or adult can take those steps right now and pass from death to life. There is nothing mysterious about coming to Jesus to be saved. Sins are forgiven by meeting the three conditions laid down in the Bible—repentance, confession, and restitution. We have reduced these long words to an equation that the most simple can understand.

We have shown that the second large step to Christ is the new-birth experience. This profound change takes place when an individual accepts Jesus as a personal substitute and Saviour. It often happens in conjunction with the imputed justification that is credited when sins are confessed. The resulting relationship of love, with its attendant obedience, fulfills the last step in the process of becoming a Christian.

If you haven't entered fully into this joyful relationship with the Lord Jesus, don't hesitate to take the three steps right now. And if there is any confusion about what to do or how to do it, just forget about protocol or procedures and tell the Lord exactly how you feel and what you desire. He will be there to lead you into the most satisfying experience you've ever imagined.